London Midland Steam

The Closing Years

Allan Heyes

LONDON

IAN ALLAN LTD

For Joan

Contents

First published 1980

ISBN 0 7110 1012 9

Published by Ian Allan Ltd, Shepperton, Surrey, and printed by Ian Allan Printing Ltd at their works at Coombelands in Runnymede, England

Introduction

The aim of this book is to create a pictorial record of the steam locomotives operating on the London Midland Region of British Railways during the last few years of steam.

The photographs, most of them taken in Lancashire, are grouped by areas. The Wigan, Preston and North-East Lancashire areas were the most familiar to me, but I have also included many pictures from other areas such as Merseyside, Chester, Bolton, Manchester, Leeds and the Settle to Carlisle route (which was formerly London Midland Region territory). Also included are a few shots of ex-LMS locomotives which operated on other regions in the 1960s; for example, some of the last Hughes /Fowler 'Crab' 2-6-0s at Ayr.

It is fitting that the last steam trains ran in Lancashire, the area where steam first firmly established its supremacy on the Liverpool & Manchester Railway. After 1830 the railway network in Lancashire was quickly established and future railway enthusiasts were provided with many fascinating venues.

The Wigan area was certainly one of the most interesting, being situated on the West Coast main line and also on important cross-country routes. The main line trains were always hampered by speed restrictions and there was no really high-speed running near Wigan. Northbound trains were also severely hampered by the 1 in 104 gradient of Boar's Head Bank, which begins at the north end of Wigan North Western station, easing off only as Standish Junction is approached. The slow passage of freight trains along this stretch of line, which is double track only, made it an operational bottleneck and for this reason some freight was diverted along the now abandoned Wigan Avoiding Line. Northbound trains left the main line at Bamfurlong, just south of Springs Branch and travelled through Whelley to rejoin the main line at Standish Junction.

The Springs Branch complex was also of great interest and a lot of steam could be seen here until the closure of the depot to steam at the end of 1967. Springs Branch locomotive rosters were mainly concerned with mineral and freight traffic and the many shunting duties at the Bamfurlong sorting sidings and other smaller yards. The coal traffic, for which the Wigan area was once famous, had greatly declined by the 1960s and at the end of steam the only coal trains originating locally were from Bickershaw Collieries, situated near the ex-LNWR line to Manchester. These trains joined the main line at Springs Branch.

Eight-coupled mineral engines were always a common sight, ex-LNWR G2 class 0-8-0s reigning supreme until the early 1960s. They were replaced by some ex-WD 2-8-0s which were in turn superseded by Stanier 2-8-0s.

Stanier 5MT 4-6-os were used on almost every type of duty, although Springs Branch did not have any regular express passenger turns. By the mid-1960s most of the remaining local passenger trains were operated by dmus and those locomotive types which had been used primarily for this purpose were withdrawn before the end of steam; eg the Stanier and Fairburn Class 4 2-6-4Ts and the Ivatt Class 2 2-6-os.

In May 1967 only six different classes of locomotive were observed in use or under repair at the depot. In steam were nine Stanier 5MT 4-6-os and eight Stanier 8F 2-8-os. Under repair were one Stanier 5MT 4-6-o, two Stanier 8F 2-8-os, three BR Standard Class 4 2-6-os and two BR Standard Class 9F 2-10-os.

The final years of steam did, however, bring more frequent appearances of some locomotive types which had previously been comparatively rare eg 'Britannia' Pacifics and the 9F 2-10-os. Nevertheless, to the lineside observer it was the older ex-LMS 5MTs and 8Fs which seemed better able to endure the neglect of these years. It seemed evident that the LMS had already achieved the reliability and robust simplicity of design which BR design staff had sought after Nationalisation.

From the platforms of Wigan North Western station, the eastern approaches to the ex-LYR Wallgate station could be observed. There was an intensive service of cross-country expresses from Yorkshire and Manchester to Liverpool and Southport, which were almost entirely in the hands of the ubiquitous 'Black 5', although Southport depot sometimes employed BR Standard Class 4 4-6-os and ex-LMS Class 4 2-6-4Ts. 'Jubilee' 4-6-os from Bank Hall or Newton Heath were also seen. These classes could also be seen on the slow trains together with Ivatt Class 2 2-6-os. The powerful Class 4 2-6-4Ts allocated to the ex-LYR lines spent much of their lives toying with three-coach trains and their acceleration away from the

frequent station stops could far outstrip the dmus which replaced them, if the driver felt so inclined. Dieselisation came early to all these services and by the mid-1960s there was very little steam operation.

The ex-LYR route to Liverpool provided much operational interest because of the rather difficult climb facing westbound trains from Pemberton Junction to Upholland Tunnel, sometimes called Orrell Bank. There is about 100yd at 1 in 39 just before Pemberton station which effectively reduced the speed of freight trains before they tackled the remaining two miles of 1 in 91 up to the tunnel.

Much of this freight came from Yorkshire and used the now-abandoned Westwood Park line from Hindley, to rejoin the line from Wallgate station at Pemberton Junction. The mainstay of this traffic was the ex-WD 2-8-o, a great number of which were allocated to ex-LYR depots. Locomotives from Wakefield, Normanton and even Goole could be seen with trains bound for various destinations on Merseyside. The descent from Upholland Tunnel towards Liverpool was probably the fastest stretch of line on the whole of the ex-LYR system. Expresses would pass through Rainford Junction at 75-80mph after descending the two and a half miles from the tunnel on a gradient averaging 1 in 120. The coming of the dmus with their maximum speed of 70mph took all the excitement out of the running over this stretch of line.

Although resident in the Wigan area until 1968, I made frequent trips to Preston. The station was formerly jointly operated by the LYR and the LNWR and this was still reflected in the traffic movements in the 1960s. Through trains from Manchester to Blackpool continued to run as in LYR days, joining the main line at Euxton Junction and taking the Blackpool line about 200yd north of Preston station. Trains from Liverpool joined the main line near Farington. Traffic from North-East Lancashire could either use the Farington Curve and gain access to any of the main line platforms, or enter the eastern (ex-LYR) side of the station. This latter approach is now dismantled.

Many of the main line trains were split at Preston, which provided great operational interest until the end of steam. Trains from Glasgow were split into Liverpool and Manchester portions. Coaches for Blackpool formed the rear portion of some trains from Euston. It was the operation of these portions which provided the steam enthusiast with regular passenger runs right up to 3 August 1968. The last two regular steam-hauled passenger trains were the 20.50 to Blackpool, which was the rear portion of the 17.05 from Euston, hauled by Class 5MT No 45212; and the 21.25 to Liverpool, a portion of the 17.25 from Glasgow, hauled by Class 5MT No 45318. The very last occasion when passengers were hauled by steam in regular service was on Sunday 4 August 1968 when Class 5MT No 45212 shunted sleeping cars off the 23.45 from Euston into a bay platform. Lostock Hall depot provided all the locomotives for these workings.

A move to North-East Lancashire in 1968 enabled me to concentrate my photographic activities in the Clitheroe, Burnley and Blackburn areas. By this time there was very little variety of motive power to be seen and anything other than a Stanier 5MT or 8F was a rare sight in this area. At Blackburn coal trains from Yorkshire to the West Coast could be seen and the return empties, the locomotives being from either the Lostock Hall or Rose Grove depots. Steam could still be seen on various shunting duties and pick-up freights. The yard at Clitheroe was still in use at this time and there was also some traffic to the Ribble Cement Works nearby. Rose Grove locomotives could be seen on these duties right up to the end of steam.

Saturday 3 August 1968 was a memorable occasion at Rose Grove. Hundreds of people were at the depot to see the locomotives returning from their last duties and it became almost an unofficial open day. On the following day five end of steam specials passed through Blackburn and four different classes of locomotive were represented. There was the last surviving 'Britannia' Pacific *Oliver Cromwell*, BR Class 5MT No 73069, six Stanier Class 5MTs and two Stanier Class 8Fs. The final steam event was the British Railways special from Liverpool to Carlisle via Ais Gill and return on the following Sunday.

Finally, a word about my approach to railway photography. There was so little variety in the locomotive types running in these final years that, like many other photographers, I have tried to get away from the conventional three-quarter front view of locomotives and trains to compose scenes which are of pictorial interest. Station buildings, bridges and other structures are often used to give perspective to the scene. This technique has also recorded many aspects of the railway landscape such as Victorian ironwork, water-towers and semaphore signals, which were so much part of the steam era. I hope that the result has been to capture not only the character of the steam locomotive, but also to re-create the environment in which it worked.

Main Line Around Wigan

Above left: **Taken from Wigan Wallgate station, this view shows Class 5MT 4-6-0s No 44962 shunting in the ex-LYR yard and No 45121 on pilot duties at the north end of the North Western station, April 1967.**

Left: **'Duchess' Pacific No 46237** *City of Bristol* **pauses at Wigan with a Carlisle-Crewe parcels train, May 1964.**

Above: **Another view from Wigan Wallgate station. Class 9F 2-10-0 No 92118 heads a northbound main line freight, June 1967.**

Right: **Class 5MT 4-6-0 No 44906 waits for the road out of Wigan with an evening Liverpool-Preston parcels train, May 1967.**

Above: 'Britannia' Pacific No 70009 *Alfred the Great* leaves Wigan with the 13.46 Barrow-Euston, June 1966.

Below: Class 5MT 4-6-0 No 44679 takes water at the south end of Wigan North Western station, May 1967.

Top: **A run-down 'Britannia' Pacific, No 70008** *Black Prince,* **leaves Wigan in pouring rain with the 13.46 Barrow-Euston, May 1966.**

Above: **Night-shift pilot duties for Class 5MT 4-6-0 No 45312 at Wigan North Western station, June 1967.**

Above: **Rebuilt 'Patriot' 4-6-0 No 45531** *Sir Frederick Harrison* **approaches Standish Junction with an up freight in July 1964. The train is signalled to take the Wigan Avoiding Line to Bamfurlong.**

Below: **'Britannia' Pacific No 70005** *John Milton* **leaves the Wigan Avoiding Line at Standish Junction with a Bidston-Euxton freight, March 1967.**

Top right: **BR Class 9F 2-10-0 No 92208 comes off the slow line at Standish Junction with a Carlisle-Margam freight in March 1967.**

Bottom right: **Class 5MT 4-6-0 No 44711 at Boar's Head Junction in July 1967 with a freight for Wyre Dock, Fleetwood. There was once a station at this point.**

Top: **Evening on Boar's Head Bank. Class 5MT 4-6-0 No 44834 climbs the 1 in 104 gradient with a down fitted freight in June 1967.**

Above: **Silhouetted against the evening sky, a 'Britannia' Pacific heads a down parcels train near Whitley, September 1966.**

Below: **An up fish train from Fleetwood coasts down the gradient at Whitley, headed by Class 5MT 4-6-0 No 44711, June 1967.**

Springs Branch mpd – 1

Left: **Class 5MT 4-6-0 No 45116 is coaled as Class 8F 2-8-0 No 48722 lies dead on an adjacent track, May 1967.**

Below: **A pair of Fairburn Class 4 2-6-4Ts, Nos 42235 and 42102, at the entrance to the repair shop, December 1965.**

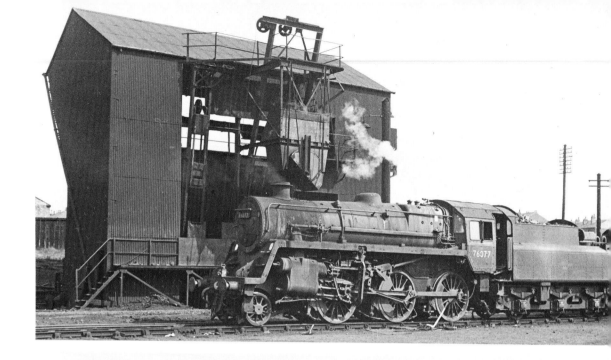

Top: **No 76077, one of Sutton Oak's Horwich-built Standard Class 4 2-6-0s at the coaling stage in August 1964.**

Above: **Ivatt Class 2 2-6-0 No 46484 in August 1964, fitted with a narrow tapered chimney. Later examples of the class reverted to the original wider design.**

Above: **Class 5MT 4-6-os Nos 45395 and 44761 outside the repair shop in November 1967. The then new diesel depot can be seen on the right.**

Left: **Class 9F 2-10-0 No 92156 receives attention to its superheater in May 1967.**

Below: **A Class 5MT 4-6-0 after collision with a parcels train at Bickershaw Junction in March 1965.**

Main Line Around Springs Branch

Left: Shortly after its last visit to Crewe Works, ex-LNWR Class G2 0-8-0 No 49451 approaches Springs Branch shed after shunting duties at Bamfurlong in June 1960.

Below left: Rebuilt 'Jubilee' 4-6-0 No 45736 *Phoenix* reverses across the main line on to the shed in June 1964.

Right: Class 5MT 4-6-0 No 44882 passes beneath the signal gantry at Springs Branch No 1 signalbox with a southbound freight in May 1967. The Manchester lines diverge to the right.

Below: Class 8F 2-8-0 No 48643 accelerates past Springs Branch with a northbound train from ICI at Northwich in May 1967.

Top left: **An Oxley-Carlisle freight, headed by rebuilt 'Patriot' 4-6-0 No 45526** *Morecambe and Heysham,* **is checked by the distant signal at Springs Branch No 1, July 1964.**

Centre left: **Rebuilt 'Patriot' 4-6-0 No 45530** *Sir Frank Ree* **heads a down afternoon parcels, July 1964.**

Bottom left: **'Britannia' Pacifics meet at Springs Branch. No 70023** *Venus* **heads a Euston-Windermere train (formerly the 'Lakes Express'). No 70028** *Royal Star* **heads a southbound freight, April 1964.**

Above: **Class 9F 2-10-0 No 92052 climbs away from Ince Moss Junction with a train of Widnes-Long Meg mineral empties in July 1967. It is about to cross over the main line and take the Wigan Avoiding Line to Standish Junction.**

Below: **Stanier Mogul No 42954 shunts the refuse sidings near Ince Moss Junction in November 1966. The last few engines of this class ended their days at Springs Branch depot.**

Top: **The evening Edge Hill-Carlisle fitted freight was a regular turn of Edge Hill's last remaining 'Duchess' Pacifics. No 46243** *City of Lancaster* **is seen here passing Ince Moss Junction in August 1964. All remaining members of the class were withdrawn in the autumn of that year.**

Above: **Stanier Mogul No 42963 and 8F 2-8-0 No 48764 pause between shunting duties at Ince Moss Junction in May 1966.**

Top right: **Another view of Stanier Mogul No 42954 near Ince Moss Junction in November 1966.**

Centre right: **Class 8F 2-8-0 No 48675 has just joined the main line at Springs Branch with a Bickershaw Collieries-Ribble Sidings coal train, May 1967.**

Bottom right: **'Jinty' 0-6-0T No 47493 near Springs Branch in July 1964.**

Above: Class 8F 2-8-0 No 48348 leaves the main line at Springs Branch with a train of empties for Bickershaw Collieries in February 1968.

Right: A clear road for 8F 2-8-0 No 48267 as it approaches the main line at Crompton's Sidings with a coal train from Bickershaw Collieries in June 1967. No 48556 moves on to Springs Branch shed.

Springs Branch mpd – 2

Left: An open smokebox door reveals the blast-pipe and superheater arrangements of an 8F 2-8-0, February 1966.

Below: An immaculate Ivatt Class 2 2-6-0, in evening sunshine at Springs Branch in May 1966. No 46517 was formerly allocated to the Western Region and still has green livery.

Bottom: BR 9F 2-10-0 No 92027 was one of 10 locomotives fitted with a Franco-Crosti boiler, but all were later converted to work conventionally. Note that the centre driving wheels are flangeless, August 1966.

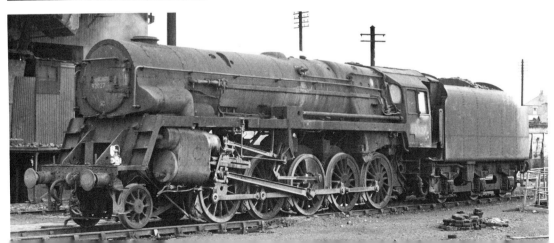

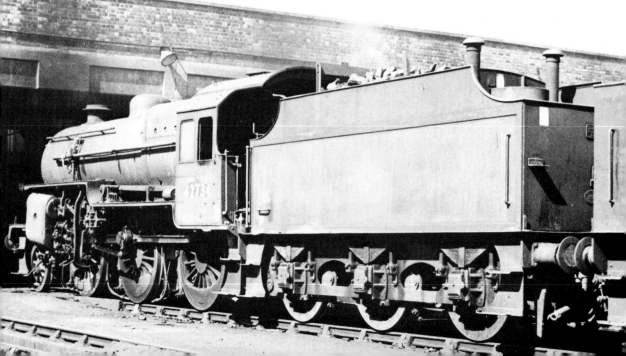

Left: **Class 8F 2-8-0 No 48275 moves off the shed in March 1967.**

Below left: **Hughes/Fowler 2-6-0 No 42734 outside the repair shop in September 1964.**

Right: **Ivatt Class 2 2-6-0 No 46515 is prepared for its journey to the scrapyard in May 1967. The connecting rods are being loaded on to the tender.**

Below: **Sunset on steam at Springs Branch in May 1967.**

Merseyside

Above: **BR Class 5MT 4-6-0 No 73140, fitted with Caprotti valve gear, awaits departure from Lime Street station with the 23.38 to York in July 1967.**

Below: **Fairburn Class 4 2-6-4T No 42235 awaits departure from Liverpool Riverside station with an enthusiasts' special organised by the Liverpool University Transport Society in October 1966.**

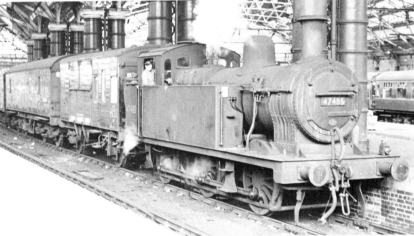

Top left The old and the new at Liverpool Lime Street in May 1964; Class 3F 0-6-0T No 47487 and electric locomotive No E3081.

Left: The Edge Hill 'Jinties' were a familiar sight at Lime Street. No 47485 is shunting parcel vehicles in May 1964.

Below: The 15.08 Southport-Euston at Edge Hill Lane Junction in June 1965, hauled by a Fairburn 2-6-4T. The two coaches will be attached to the Liverpool-London portion at Lime Street station.

Above: **Kingmoor 9F 2-10-0s were a familiar sight on the Long Meg-Widnes anhydrite trains. Here No 92012 is seen leaving St Helens in June 1965.**

Below: **One of Sutton Oak's last 4F 0-6-0s, No 44075 shunts the yard near Shaw Street station, St Helens in June 1965.**

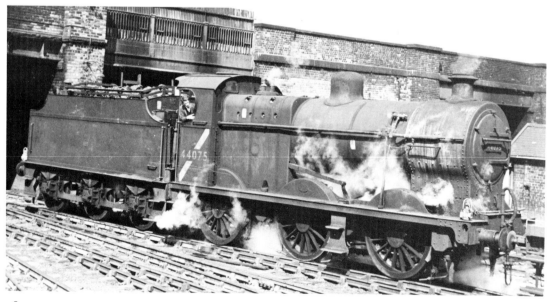

Chester

Top: **Afternoon siesta for 'Jinty' 0-6-0T No 47507 at Chester in August 1966.**

Above: **Class 5MT 4-6-0 No 44993 pauses at the western end of Chester General station with a through freight in March 1967.**

North-East Lancashire – 1

Left: Wet platforms at Blackburn as Class 8F 2-8-0 No 48493 enters the station with an eastbound train of empties, July 1968.

Below left: Torrential rain (hence the spots on the photograph!) as Class 5MT 4-6-0 No 45212 passes through Blackburn with a train of coal empties for Yorkshire in July 1968. This locomotive was the last to haul passengers in regular service and is now running on the Keighley & Worth Valley Railway.

Right: Class 8F 2-8-0 No 48340 at Hoghton, on the Blackburn-Preston line, with a coal train from Yorkshire in July 1968.

Below: The Long Meg-Widnes anhydrite train at Whalley in October 1967. English Electric Type 4 diesel No D224 requires assistance from Class 5MT 4-6-0 No 44800 up the 1 in 82 gradient to Wilpshire.

Left: **Class 5MT 4-6-0 No 45297 coasts down the gradient between Wilpshire and Whalley with the daily pick-up freight to Clitheroe in July 1968.**

Below left **Class 8F 2-8-0 No 48081 and reflections in the yard at Clitheroe, November 1967.**

Right: **A busy midday scene at Clitheroe in February 1967 with 8F 2-8-0 No 48313 and Class 4 2-6-4T No 42297 on shunting duties. The 2-6-4Ts were seldom seen on goods trains.**

Below: **Another view of No 48081, this time through the remains of the Clitheroe goods shed.**

Below right: **No 42297 takes water at Clitheroe.**

33

Above: Viewed from the castle, Class 8F 2-8-0 No 48348 shunts the goods yard at Clitheroe, February 1968.

Left: Class A3 Pacific *Flying Scotsman* has just arrived at Accrington on an enthusiasts' special. It will be replaced by Class 5MT No 44899, seen in the distance, March 1968.

Top right: An unusual view (apart from the rain, that is) of No 45156 at Blackburn in July 1968.

Top far right: Class 8F 2-8-0 No 48775 ambles into Blackburn with a short freight in July 1968. This was one of three locomotives (Nos 48773-5) returned from WD stock in 1957. They were easily recognised by their large top-feed casing.

Right: Class 5MT 4-6-0 No 45156, formerly named *Ayrshire Yeomanry*, at Blackburn in July 1968.

Above left **Class 8F 2-8-0 No 48384 enters Blackburn station with an eastbound train of coal empties in February 1968.**

Left: **Fairburn Class 4 2-6-4T No 42187, returning light-engine to Lostock Hall, rounds the sharp curve through Accrington station in April 1967.**

Above: **A line-up of Stanier locomotives at Rose Grove depot, Burnley in May 1968.**

Right: **Class 8F 2-8-0 No 48257, fitted with a snowplough, inside Rose Grove mpd, May 1968.**

North of Tebay

Above: **Class 5MT 4-6-0 No 45421 coasts down the 1 in 75 gradient at Scout Green with a parcels train in August 1966.**

Below: **BR 5MT 4-6-0 No 73127, with Caprotti valve gear, passes Shap Wells in August 1966 with a northbound freight.**

Top: A pleasant June evening in 1967 at Carlisle Kingmoor as Class 5MT 4-6-0 No 44792 heads an up freight.

Above: The south end of the Kingmoor complex, with Class 5MT 4-6-0 No 45454 on a down freight in July 1967.

Right: Class 9F 2-10-0 No 92051 catches the June evening sunlight at the northern end of Kingmoor mpd in 1967.

Below: 'Crab' 2-6-0 No 42919 uses the rather antiquated coaling facilities at Ayr mpd in August 1966.

Cross-Country Routes in the Wigan Area

Left: **Stanier 'Black 5' No 45156, formerly named** *Ayrshire Yeomanry*, **hurries light-engine past Hindley North in December 1967.**

Below: **Many of the Class 5MTs fitted with Caprotti valve gear spent their last months working between Southport, Rochdale, Manchester and Liverpool. Here, in September 1965 No 44757 fitted with double chimney is crossing the Leeds-Liverpool Canal at Martland Mill with the 16.10 Manchester-Southport.**

Above: **A Long Meg-Widnes anhydrite train climbs the gradient between Springs Branch and Bryn in July 1964. Class 9F 2-10-0 No 92023 formerly had a Franco-Crosti boiler. A WD 2-8-0 is the banker, July 1964.**

Below: **BR Class 4 2-6-0 No 76079 sets off from Old Mill Lane, on the Rainford Junction-St Helens branch, with a sand train for Pilkington's glass works, St Helens in May 1965.**

Top: **Class 5MT 4-6-0 No 44809 emerges from Upholland Tunnel and begins the three-mile descent into Wigan with the daily Fazakerley-Bamfurlong freight, December 1966.**

Above: **Fowler Class 4 2-6-4T No 42374 enters the 959yd Upholland Tunnel with the 18.05 Liverpool-Wigan in July 1965.**

Above: **Ex-LNW Class G2 0-8-0 No 49335 takes water in the goods loop at Winstanley Colliery Sidings, April 1961.**

Below: **Class 8F 2-8-0 No 48676 passes Winstanely Colliery Sidings with a Bamfurlong-Fazakerley freight in March 1967.**

Top: **Again photographed at Winstanley, No 48676 is on the return working to Bamfurlong on the same day.**

Above: **Stanier Class 4 2-6-4T No 42611 climbs the 1 in 90 gradient approaching Pemberton Junction with the 12.15 Wigan-Liverpool stopping train in September 1965.**

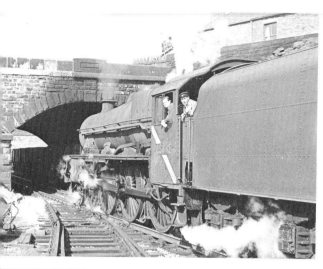

Above left: 'Jubilee' 4-6-0 No **45642** *Boscawen* restarts the 09.50 Bolton-Liverpool Exchange from Pemberton in August 1964.

Left: Wakefield WD 8F 2-8-0 No **90074** at Pemberton with a Fazakerley-Crofton empties in August 1964. The train will take the Wigan Avoiding Line from Pemberton Junction to Hindley.

Below: Ivatt Class 2 2-6-0 No **46419** accelerates smartly down the short 1 in 39 gradient at Pemberton Junction with the 11.40 all-stations Liverpool-Wigan Wallgate, August 1964.

Right: Ivatt Class 2 2-6-0 No **46414** approaches Rainford Junction with the 18.56 Liverpool Exchange-Manchester Victoria stopping train in July 1965.

Below right: WD 2-8-0 No **90405** labours up the 1 in 116 gradient through Upholland with a Fazakerley-Crofton empties in April 1964.

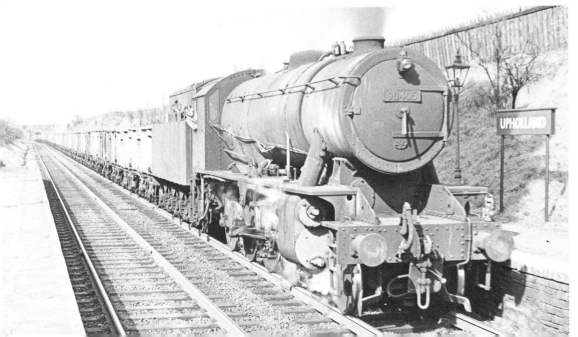

Above: Another view of the eastern end of Upholland Tunnel taken in August 1964. WD 2-8-0 No 90333 is in charge of the Crofton empties.

Left: Stanier Mogul No 42968 at Whelley Junction on a brake-van tour of the Wigan area in August 1966. The locomotive is standing on the single-track spur between Whelley Junction and Red Rock.

Above right: Stanier Class 4 2-6-4T No 42631 pauses at Hindley South with the 14.00 Wigan Central-Manchester Central in July 1964.

Right: Stanier Class 4 2-6-4T No 42426 at Bickershaw & Abram with the 14.12 (SO) Irlam-Wigan Central in October 1964.

Ex-LYR Lines in Lancashire

Above left: Class 5MT 4-6-0 No 44736 takes the through road at Bolton Trinity Street with the 07.25 Blackpool-Manchester express in September 1966.

Left: A pause between shunting duties at Bolton Trinity Street in April 1967 for BR Class 2MT 2-6-0 No 78012.

Above: Class 5MT 4-6-0 No 44709 passes Bolton West with a freight for Brindle Heath Sidings, Manchester, in May 1968.

Right: Another view of No 44709, entering the road bridge which spans the western end of Bolton station.

Far left: Class 5MT No 44664 inside the repair shop at Bolton mpd in June 1967.

Left: Stanier Class 8F 2-8-0 No 48425, at Bolton mpd in March 1967, is dwarfed by the coaling plant.

Below left: Class 5MT 4-6-0 No 45404 looks unfit for service at Bolton mpd, March 1967.

Above: 'Jubilee' class 4-6-0 No 45562 *Alberta*, in surprisingly rural surroundings about $1\frac{1}{2}$ miles from the centre of Bolton, approaches Lostock Junction with an enthusiasts' special in October 1967.

Below: Class 5MT 4-6-0 No 45073 passes through Platform 1 at Bolton with a brake van in May 1968.

Right: Class 8F 2-8-0 No 48425 passes through Bolton as a dmu awaits departure on a Rochdale train, June 1967.

Below: A coal train from NCB sidings approaches the BR yard at Kearsley behind Class 8F 2-8-0 No 48534 in March 1967.

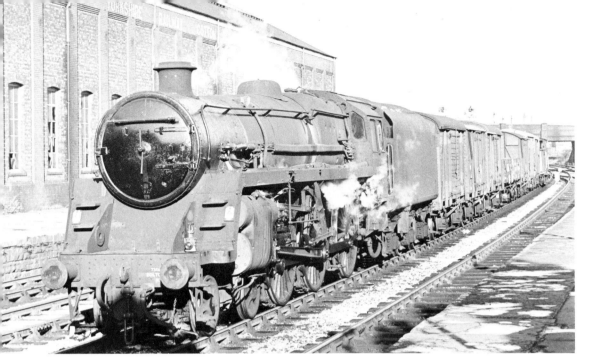

Above: BR Class 5MT 4-6-0 No 73156 passes through Bury Knowsley Street with a local freight to Bolton, April 1967.

Left: Class 8F 2-8-0 No 48740 tops the rise to Bury Knowsley Street station in April 1967 with an eastbound fitted freight.

Below left: BR Class 5MT 4-6-0 No 73045 alongside the famous No 11 Platform at Manchester Victoria on a parcels train in July 1967. This view shows the continuation of the platform to the now-closed Exchange station.

Above: **Contrasts in architectural styles in Manchester, as Class 8F 2-8-0 No 48090 passes light-engine through Victoria station, June 1967.**

Left: **A down parcels train awaits departure from Manchester Victoria in June 1967 behind Class 5MT 4-6-0 No 44938.**

Above right: **Fowler Dock Tank 0-6-0T No 47165 on shunting duties near Horwich Locomotive Works in July 1964.**

Right: **The last of the ex-LYR 0-6-0 saddle tanks were used on shunting duties around Horwich Locomotive Works. No 11305 was built in 1877 as a tender locomotive, rebuilt in 1891 as a saddletank and withdrawn in September 1964, a month after this photograph was taken.**

Top: **Fowler Class 4 2-6-4T No 42369 enters Banks with the 08.50 Southport-Preston local. This line was closed a few days after this photograph was taken in September 1964.**

Above: **BR Class 4MT 4-6-0 No 75047 on a Preston-Liverpool express in June 1965, scoops water from the troughs near Burscough.**

The Preston Area

Above: **Class 5MT 4-6-0 No 45149 prepares to leave Preston in May 1967 with the 12.44 to Blackpool North. The train is the rear portion of the 09.05 from Euston.**

Below: **BR Class 9F 2-10-0 No 92110 avoids the platform roads at Preston with a northbound freight in September 1967.**

Above: A 'Wakes' special from Wigan to Blackpool in July 1967 leaves Preston behind Class 5MT 4-6-0 No 45310.

Left: 'Britannia' Pacific No 70029 *Shooting Star* stops at Preston with the 13.46 Barrow-Euston in September 1966.

Below left: A coal train from Yorkshire enters Preston by the East Lancashire lines in September 1966, headed by WD 2-8-0 No 90047. This approach is now dismantled.

Top right: Looking through the bridge at the north end of Preston Station, Class 8F 2-8-0 No 48646 is seen taking water in September 1967.

Centre right: A southbound freight climbs out of Preston, towards Farington, behind Class 8F 2-8-0 No 48700 in May 1967.

Bottom right: A light load for 'Jubilee' class No 45675 *Hardy* on the up fast line at Euxton Junction in July 1964.

Above: **'Royal Scot' class No 46118** *Royal Welch Fusilier* **heads a Carlisle-Crewe parcels train near Coppull, March 1964.**

Right: **Holiday specials in May 1967 await departure from Blackpool North for Accrington. Ivatt Class 4 2-6-0 No 43004 is on the 20.05 (left) and Class 5MT 4-6-0 No 45056 is on the 19.20, May 1967.**

Below right: **Ivatt Class 4 2-6-0 No 43029 is on pilot duty at Preston as Class 5MT No 45092 prepares to leave with a southbound parcels train in May 1967.**

62

Above: Diesel shunter No D4114 receives attention at Preston in September 1967 as 'Britannia' Pacific No 70028 *Royal Star* leaves on a Carlisle-Crewe parcels.

Left: Class 5MT 4-6-0 No 45057 is about to take the 12.15 to Manchester out of Preston in May 1967.

Left: BR 9F 2-10-0 No 92233 takes the up fast line from Preston with a fitted freight in September 1966.

Below: Class 5MT 4-6-0 No 45450 makes a vigorous start from Preston with a northbound special in July 1967.

Right: Fairburn Class 4 2-6-4T shunts empty stock at Preston, September 1966.

Below right: 'Britannia' Pacific No 70045 *Lord Rowallan* at Preston shortly before departure with a Carlisle train in September 1967.

Above: Sleeping cars, which will be attached to the 22.36 to Euston, are warmed by Ivatt Class 4 2-6-0 No 43119 at Preston July 1967.

Left: Seen through the road bridge at the north end of Preston station in May, 1967 WD 2-8-0 No 90650 restarts a coal train.

Above right: BR Class 2MT 2-6-0 No 78037, a 'Jinty' and another 78XXX at Lostock Hall mpd in October 1965.

Right: Two of the last survivors at Lostock Hall mpd in July 1968 were Class 5MT 4-6-0 No 45231 and 8F 2-8-0 No 48775.

Right: **Careful attention for a 'Black 5' at Lostock Hall mpd in preparation for an end of steam special in July 1968.**

Below: **May 1967 was the end of the line for this group of locomotives at Lostock Hall mpd.**

Inside the Holbeck Roundhouse in June 1967

Above: **A pair of 'Jubilee' class 4-6-0s. No 45593** *Kolhapur* **is in steam; No 45697** *Achilles* **is under repair.**

Left: **Class 5MT 4-6-0 No 44912 moves off the turntable.**

Below left: **Class 5MT 4-6-0 No 44852 and Fairburn Class 4 2-6-4T No 42152.**

Yorkshire and the North-East

Above: Type 2 diesel No D5175 and Fairburn Class 4 2-6-4T No 42689 prepare to leave Leeds City with the 10.38 to Bradford in June 1967.

Right: The Ivatt Class 4 2-6-os were virtually adopted as a BR Standard design before the appearance of the 75XXX series. Here No 43015 is seen on West Hartlepool shed in June 1967 with Q6 class 0-8-0 No 63394 in the foreground.

Above left: Fairburn Class 4 2-6-4T No 42689 and Type 2 diesel No D5177 back on to the Bradford portion of a Kings Cross-Bradford train at Leeds City, July 1967.

Left: No 42574, one of the last Stanier Class 4 2-6-4Ts, on pilot duties at Normanton in July 1967.

Below: 'Jubilee' class 4-6-0 No 45562 *Alberta*, working an up freight, is checked by signals at Skipton. May 1967.

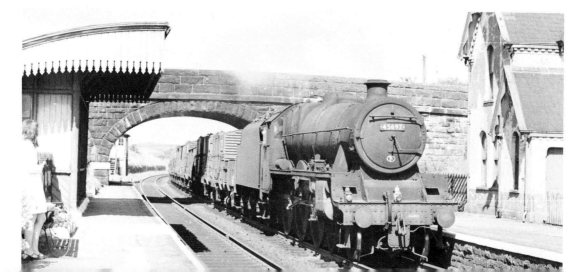

Above: **Another view of** *Alberta* **at Skipton. On the left Ivatt Class 4 2-6-0 No 43105 is taking the Grassington branch with a short freight.**

Below: **An up freight passes through Long Preston behind 'Jubilee' class 4-6-0 No 45697** *Achilles* **in August 1966.**

Top right: **BR Class 9F 2-10-0 No 92233 heads a southbound mineral train through Long Preston in August 1966.** *Joan Heyes*

Centre right: **A Stanier Class 8F 2-8-0 on the 'Long Drag' in July 1967. No 48646 is approaching Ribblehead Viaduct.**

Bottom right: **'Britannia' Pacific No 70024** *Vulcan* **approaches Ribblehead station with an up freight, July 1967.**

Right: **A short freight pauses in the up loop at Blea Moor in July 1967 headed by 'Britannia' Pacific No 70035** *Rudyard Kipling.*

Below: **Class 8F 2-8-0 No 48646 labours over Ribblehead Viaduct with a northbound freight in July 1967.**

North-East Lancashire – Finale, 1968

Above: An 8F 2-8-0 shunts the yard at Rose Grove on 3 August as another 8F enters the shed after its last duty as a Copy Pit banker.

Below: Class 8F 2-8-0 enters the coaling plant at Rose Grove mpd on 3 August.

Right: No 48773 under the coaling plant.

Below: No 48773 moves away from the coaling plant and is now ready to work one of the end of steam specials on the following day.

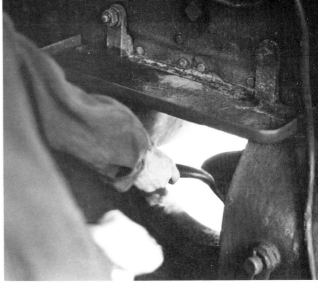

Left: A view from the footplate of Class 8F 2-8-0 No 48723 shunting the coal sidings at Clitheroe in July.

Above: Firing 8F No 48723.

Below: Class 8F 2-8-0 No 48723 crosses the River Calder at Whalley in July. It is returning to Blackburn with the daily Blackburn-Clitheroe pick-up freight.

Right: A SLS special from Birmingham enters Blackburn on 4 August hauled by Stanier 5MT 4-6-0s Nos 44871 and 44894.

Below: Another SLS special from Birmingham on 4 August takes water at the western end of Blackburn station. The front engine is Class 5MT 4-6-0 No 44874 and the train engine is No 45017.

Above: **An unusual combination of motive power for the RCTS special from Manchester Victoria to Hellifield. Class 8F 2-8-0 No 48476 is double-heading with BR Standard Class 5MT No 73069 on 4 August.**

Left: **Class 8F 2-8-0 No 48773 and Class 5MT 4-6-0 No 44781 leave Blackburn on 4 August with the LCGB special from St Pancras to Carnforth.**

Rose Grove, 3 August.